Hearts in HEALING

A Devotional Journey from Battling
Trials to Realizing Blessings

Molly Hankey

WESTBOW
PRESS®
A DIVISION OF THOMAS NELSON
& ZONDERVAN

WestBow Press books may be ordered through booksellers or by contacting:

WestBow Press
A Division of Thomas Nelson & Zondervan
1663 Liberty Drive
Bloomington, IN 47403
www.westbowpress.com
844-714-3454

ISBN: 978-1-6642-4243-2 (sc)
ISBN: 978-1-6642-4245-6 (hc)
ISBN: 978-1-6642-4244-9 (e)

Library of Congress Control Number: 2021916200

Print information available on the last page.

WestBow Press rev. date: 11/17/2021

CONTENTS

PREFACE

Life is a journey.
Life is a carrousel.
Life is a highway.

A few years ago, my family visited the Great Smokey Mountains in Tennessee for a summer vacation. In the mountains of Pigeon Forge, we discovered an alpine roller coaster. It was a cross between a roller coaster and one of those big carnival slides where you sit in a burlap bag. It was operated by weight and gravity but on rails that twisted, turned, rose up, and dipped down over and through the natural terrain. It was a mountaintop-to-valley ride through serene forest, past majestic boulders, amid patches of thorns, by way of sunlight and shadow, bringing delight yet furnishing the stomach-in-the-throat sensation as the speed increased and flying offtrack felt inevitable … yet through the engineer's design was impossible.

To me, life is an alpine roller coaster.

God's design for life is *not* for it to be one blissfully glorious season after another. That's common knowledge.

Life *is* God's beautiful creation for us, but we can sometimes only see the thorns around us or boulders ahead of us that we think will be our demise. If we hang on though and trust that He's got a hold of us, He'll eventually bring us to that glorious revelation we long for. I'm not just talking about heaven; I'm talking about the sunlit, radiant joy and peace He brings us to after we've gone through a deep, dark patch of thorny thicket.

Much of my adult life has been filled with extreme highs and tremendous lows that God has used to teach me and to heal my sinful-born heart. Having a child with an abnormal physiology is just one way He teaches me His lessons and brings me closer to Him. It accounts for only portions of my alpine roller coaster. I'm sure the trial you are facing right now accounts for only portions of yours as well.

The bends and bumps caused by some kinds of burdens are lifelong. As there will always need to be physical work done on my daughter's heart, there will always be spiritual work to be done in mine. Our up-and-down ride is in progress until the day we meet our Maker ... until the day He reveals to us that *final* glorious revelation. Until then, we trust our hearts to His healing.

How about you? Will you trust that God's track won't derail you? Will you trust your heart with His unexpected plan and seek His incomprehensible healing? Will you step toward the light in faith or away from Him into darkness?

My hope and prayer as you read on is that you find encouragement in your journey, trial, or pain, as well as inspiration to make intentional choices to step closer to our Lord through your own adversities.

1

BLESSING IN DISGUISE

About two and a half minutes after the double lines on the pregnancy test revealed themselves, after the initial unintelligible words of joy erupted from my mouth and slight disbelief subsided, an innate, maternal instinct crossed my mind. *What if there's something wrong with this baby?*

I had battled anxiety through my teens and twenties and pushed this notion away, categorizing it as my well-known enemy. No, this was a time to celebrate, not worry about something there was no possible answer to right now. Yet the thought repeatedly slithered back into my mind as I shared the jubilant news of pregnancy with my husband, Jim, and our parents, family, and friends. Like a pesky weed with unreachable roots, this thought surfaced on and off for the first twenty-two weeks of my pregnancy and robbed the beautiful fruit of elation I should have been enjoying.

I'm now thankful for that early-on consideration, which somehow lessened the horrendous shock of that fateful ultrasound appointment that lay ahead. Now I know that little notion was from God and not my own anxiety-driven imagination. It was a tool that forced me to imagine my life in a different way from how I was originally hoping it would turn out. *I imagined having a disabled child.* God forced me to think about and to pray through this and come somewhat to a peace of understanding that this was a possibility and I could survive it.

What concern do you have that you want to bury? Some concerns are completely unfounded and born simply from anxiety. But maybe God has given a particular notion to you as a tool—a blessing in disguise. Through prayer and holding onto His truth and promises, we can sort out our anxieties to determine what thoughts are God inspired.

There is no time like the present to pray through your anxieties. I encourage you to ask God for clarity, wisdom, and guidance. Listen to Him speaking to your heart and receive His instruction on how to handle your concern. He promises to transform your fears into confidence.

> So do not fear, for I am with you;
> do not be dismayed, for I am your God.
> I will strengthen you and help you;
> I will uphold you with My righteous hand.
> (Isaiah 41:10 NIV)

Still your mind. Listen for the Lord. Write your prayer and the wisdom that God is speaking into your heart as you listen for His counseling.

_____

_____

_____

_____

_____

_____

_____

_____

2

Overwhelming Emotion

A late-Friday-afternoon ultrasound revealed our baby was a girl—and that there were abnormalities in her brain. The doctor dismissed it, stating that most of these abnormalities clear up in time with no effect on the baby. Regardless, the discovery didn't sit well with us. After a tiresome weekend of worry, prayer, and endless thought, we decided to request a second opinion.

At twenty-two weeks of pregnancy, we went through a more in-depth ultrasound at a special fetal-maternal-medicine clinic. Launch the roller coaster.

The technician gave us good news that Joelle's brain abnormalities had normalized.

Relief. Delight. Joy.

He moved on to exploring Joelle's heart measurements and became troubled. He called his senior staff into the ultrasound room to take a second look. After some examination, they both exited the room.

Intensity. Prayer. Angst.

We were escorted into a conference room and waited for the senior doctor to come speak with us. Breathing was a challenge, as there seemed to be very little air in that room.

Finally, he came in and sat down across the table. With lack of emotion, he said, "We are sorry to inform you that your baby has a very rare congenital heart defect. This type of heart defect is commonly seen in people that have DiGeorge syndrome, a disorder caused by chromosomal abnormalities. It can cause a myriad of disabilities. However, to confirm or disconfirm this genetic disorder, you would need to undergo an amniocentesis; this comes with risk to the pregnancy. The heart defect will also require surgery when the baby is born."

Heartbreak. Silence. Tears.

He added, "If you wish to continue the pregnancy, we will give you referrals to specialists."

What? Blinking my eyes and trying to absorb the situation, I said, "Of course we do. Of course we wish to continue the pregnancy."

We were given some doctor referrals and were offered as much time as we needed in the conference room to process our emotions.

I don't remember the car ride home, but I know it was blurred with tears. I must have called my parents because they were already at our house when we got there. Jim decided to go deliver the news to his mother in person. I sat between my parents on the sofa, in their embrace, still trying to wrap my head around the crisis.

Devastation. Confusion. Prayer.

God enabled Jim and me to find some calm and make a major decision that day, even amid our despair. We decided to forego the amniocentesis because we didn't want to put Joelle at risk, no matter the result of the genetic testing. If she did have a genetic disorder, we would love her the same as if she didn't. We would just have to wait the remainder of the pregnancy to find out the extent of her condition.

Uncertainty. Melancholy. Helplessness.

Our all-knowing Father knows every emotion that we are feeling at every moment. He created those emotions, and He created us. He desires to be praised and thanked with a heart of gratitude when He blesses us with joyous events. And He longs for us to come to Him for help in difficult and unbearable circumstances.

Often, we are so overcome with our emotions in heartbreaking situations that we forget to come to the feet of Jesus to find consolation and direction. Have you poured out your heart, crying to the Lord for help in your distress?

Hear my cry for mercy as I call to you for help, as I lift up my hands toward your Most Holy Place. (Psalm 28:2 NIV)

Journal your raw and unbridled plea to God for relief and describe any comfort He has given in response to your prayer.

_____

_____

_____

_____

_____

_____

_____

_____

_____

_____

_____

_____

_____

_____

_____

3

PRAISE THROUGH THE STORM

There was no question that Jim and I would continue to praise the Lord through this new trial, no matter the outcome. This was not the first trial we faced together in our marriage. We knew the only way we were going to get through this mentally and emotionally was to let God take us through it and trust Him to carry us. So, we would thank Him and praise Him, no matter what.

People didn't understand how we could be "so strong." We were told a lot that we were inspiring, which I never understood and still don't. We weren't strong; we were simply relying on God to carry us and praising Him for it. Like the famous "Footprints" poem, Jesus carried us because we couldn't move ourselves.

I adopted a theme song shortly after the fateful ultrasound day: "Praise You in This Storm" by Casting Crowns. Below are lyrics from the chorus.

> And I will lift my hands
> That you are who you are
> No matter where I am
> And every tear I've cried
> You hold in your hand
> You never left my side
> And though my heart is torn
> I will praise you in this storm.

Many, *many* times during the pregnancy, I sat in the driver's seat of my car, with one hand on the wheel and one hand on my growing belly, tears streaming down my face, whispering along with this song on the stereo because I just couldn't choke out the words. I'm sure people wouldn't have thought I was strong then—or inspiring. But God was strong. He still is and always will be.

Surrender to Him. Are you letting God carry you through your trial, or are you trying to walk through it alone on your own power? By God's life design, you *can't* walk through valleys alone and come out whole and bettered on the other side. He wants us to surrender our hearts and our hardships so He can heal us and grow us. Have you surrendered your heart to Him and the ordeal you are facing?

Petition Him. In surrendering our hearts, we can ask God for clarity—the reason or purpose for our pain. He allows pain in our lives as a tool to teach us about Himself and to strengthen our relationships with Him. Have you asked Him to reveal what He wants you to learn? Have you pleaded to Him for wisdom or simply deliverance from your pain?

Praise Him. When all we feel is agony, it is easy to forget the praise in our prayers. King David's words in Psalms 6 and 13 give us good examples of acknowledging God's goodness amid pain.

> Be merciful to me Lord, for I am faint;
> O Lord, heal me for my bones are in agony. My soul is in anguish.
> How long O Lord, how long?
> Turn, O Lord, and deliver me; save me because of your unfailing love. (Psalm 6:2–4 NIV)

> But I trust in Your unfailing love; my heart rejoices in your salvation.
> I will sing to the Lord, for He has been good to me. (Psalm 13:5–6 NIV)

Take a quiet moment now to surrender; acknowledge God for being in control and holding the outcome of this phase of life you are living in.

MOLLY HANKEY

Ask Him to impart His wisdom and clarity. Thank God for who He is and for the good things He has given you. Praise Him for His divine will, unfailing love, and gift of salvation.

_____

_____

_____

_____

_____

_____

_____

_____

_____

_____

_____

_____

_____

_____

_____

_____

4

LET CHRIST'S BODY DO ITS WORK

Not yet swept into the world of Facebook, we created a mass email to our family and friends, informing them of our news and requesting prayer. Here is an excerpt from that email:

> We are preparing ourselves for this. We are also praying for a miracle—God's divine healing. We know He can do anything. We have seen unbelievable things happen before, and we truly believe that He can heal Joelle and make her "perfect" before she is born. We actually chose her name a few months ago, before we knew any of this. Joelle is Hebrew, meaning "God is Willing." We are hoping that He is willing to heal her. However, we know that this might not be in His plan, which is greater than we will ever understand. So, we are praying also for His will to be done, for His strength to get us all through this, and His peace to accept it …
>
> We don't want pity, just prayers and support. Please pray vigilantly, with all your heart, for a miracle for Joelle, but also for God's will to be done. And please pray for us.

We asked that our prayer request be passed on to every prayer warrior that anyone knew and for it to be put on every prayer chain anyone was connected to. My father printed the email in bulk and took it to every church he could find in our town.

Our pastor at that time suggested a special congregational prayer with laying on of hands during our Sunday service. I wasn't initially keen on that idea. *I don't even know all the people in my church, and you want me to stand up in front of them? Of course there are people with worse problems than mine. I don't want to offend them with this. I don't feel worthy of the attention.*

In pastoral wisdom, he suggested that this was an opportunity for the body of Christ to work as it should. He asked us to let others unite in Christ, to pray us through this. The power of prayer is undefinable, and sharing this opportunity with our congregation would benefit not only us but also the body.

We agreed somewhat hesitantly but found out quickly that it was the right decision. The response of our congregation that Sunday morning was overwhelming. Five hundred brothers and sisters in Christ, out of their seats, laying hands on us by touching the shoulders of those in front of them. I just couldn't fathom the support we received that day. Of course, we were highly emotional anyway, but this brought unstoppable tears to my eyes. We *felt* the prayers of our family, our church, friends, friends of friends, and strangers we had never met. I *felt* the Holy Spirit wrapping me in peace.

The first Christians united in prayer (Acts 2:42), which was such an important part of bonding the early church together. Sometimes it's uncomfortable stepping into the center of attention, and we might feel unworthy of asking others to pray for our needs. I encourage you to let go of that fear and step into the true Christian fellowship of believers. It will bring your circle closer to one another and closer to Jesus, which is a win for everyone. And when your heart becomes too exhausted by your circumstances to utter anything to God, your fellow prayer warriors will be lifting you up.

While the apostle Paul was imprisoned in Rome for the preaching of his faith in Jesus, he wrote to his Christian brothers and sisters in Philippi:

For I know that through your prayers and the help given by the Spirit of Jesus Christ, what has happened to me will turn out for my deliverance. (Philippians 1:19 NIV)

Paul knew he needed the prayers of his fellow believers to summon God on his behalf. Are you open to giving the body of Christ the opportunity to do its work? Will you drop your defenses and tear down your walls to let others into your world, uniting in Christ to pray you through your trial?

List the people you can ask to pray for you in your time of need. I urge you to share your needs with these fellow Christians.

_____

_____

_____

_____

_____

_____

_____

_____

_____

_____

_____

_____

5

EXTRAORDINARY FOR JESUS

Our pastor asked us what our specific prayer was. My prayer above all, even to this day, is that Joelle's life will be extraordinary for the Lord—that He will use her in a great way for His glory. Of course, at that time, I was praying fervently for divine healing, but most importantly for God's will to be accomplished in an extraordinary way.

The pastor asked us to recall another child in our congregation who was severely physically disabled and asked us if we had ever interacted with her. Of course we had; everyone in our eight-hundred-person congregation knows her and her amazing family that just radiates Jesus. They don't blend in. *Oh … lightbulb!* Now I was understanding where he was going with this.

Perhaps God's plan isn't for Joelle to be divinely healed. Maybe her disability, however it manifests, is what He will use for her life to be extraordinary and to show more people His Light. If she's "normal," she'll blend in. If she stands out, more people will see God's glory in how He touches her life.

Ten years later, we have seen time and again how this has held so true. Joelle *is* different from other kids. We *do* deal with things other families don't have to deal with. God has shown and continues to show His mighty power and goodness through her and our family, which we wouldn't have experienced had He made Joelle from a normal physiological mold. Her life has already been extraordinary for Jesus, and I know in my heart He has more extraordinary things to lead her (and us) through.

The apostle Paul writes in his second letter to the church people of Corinth about his own "thorn in his flesh," which He pleaded with God to take from him. But God's reply was "My power is made perfect in weakness" (2 Corinthians 12:7–10 NIV). Paul learned to revel in his hardships and difficulties so that Christ's power could be shown through him.

Embracing our sufferings is a bitter pill to swallow, but often that's what God uses to draw us nearer to Him and to show His glory through us to those around us.

Will you try that perspective with me? I don't know what you are going through right now; it's probably a far worse situation than this particular trial I faced. Nevertheless, will you thank God for the opportunity your pain and problems present for Him to work in and through you?

If you will use your valleys to let the light of Jesus shine through you, He *will* do extraordinary things through you. That is one of His extraordinary promises.

Record your thoughts and what God is speaking to your heart:

_____

_____

_____

_____

_____

_____

_____

_____

6

VOICE OF THE SPIRIT

Even before I became pregnant, Jim and I liked the name Jocelyn and had planned to use it if we had a daughter. At twelve weeks of pregnancy, before we found out the gender of our unborn baby, we came across the name Joelle. We had heard this name before but were just now drawn to it. We appreciated the Hebrew origin and godly meaning and decided to use it instead of Jocelyn. On our Google search, we found Joelle to mean "God is willing." I didn't know what that meant for her at the time (I didn't even know we were having a girl), although I was very curious. Because we had felt so led to this name, like God had directed us to it, I had an idea that this was more than just a name; it was a prophetic birthright.

Three months later, after finding out about the issues Joelle had and might have, and after nearly endless prayer, we sat in church during a Sunday sermon, listening to our pastor speak. During the message, our pastor said, "Ask Him. God *is* willing!" Both at attention, Jim and I looked at each other knowingly, without the need of spoken word, and felt the Holy Spirit overcome us with a tingle from head to toe. The depth behind Jim's eyes understood and agreed with the expression on my face that said, "That's her name. That's her legacy. God *is* willing to heal her!"

I grabbed up a CD copy of the recorded sermon that day, anxious to hear those words—God *is* willing!—over and over again. I thought I had gotten distracted the first time I played it, and I missed hearing the words. I listened more closely the second time and the third. The words weren't there. I listened intently to every single word on that CD, from start to finish, and the words I craved so deeply to hear had disappeared from history like a mysterious vapor.

Jim and I came to the conclusion that we heard God's Holy Spirit speak to us that day in an audible voice, through our pastor. In speaking with him about it, he confirmed the phrase "God is willing" was not part of his message. Although he didn't have any abnormal sensations or feel anything remarkable overcome him that Sunday morning, he responded, "It certainly could have happened. Anything is possible with God."

Needless to say, we believe that's true—*anything is possible with God*. We know we physically heard the Lord speak to us that day. Beyond being astounded by that alone, we were given peace, excitement, contentment, and hope from those words. It let us know again that God was *with* us in this journey. He was hearing our prayers. He was seeing our struggle. He was with us.

Sometimes we get significant, tangible signs from God to guide us or to let us know that He is near. Jim and I were fortunate to receive that at that particular time of our journey. But many times, those signs don't come. So often, we pray for the Lord's direction and hope for an obvious sign from Him without receiving one. That doesn't mean He's not listening, walking with us, and guiding us.

It is in these times where God speaks softly and quietly to our hearts. After we pour out all of our petitions and praises to Him, He wants us to quiet our hearts and minds before Him so we can listen for His response. It is then that we are able to feel His Spirit guiding us from within.

I like to visually place myself at the feet of Jesus on His throne in heaven when I am in deepest and most worshipful prayer. It gives me an image to meditate on while I quietly listen for His wisdom to seep into my thoughts and my heart.

> The Lord is near to all who call on Him; to all who call on Him in truth. (Psalm 145:18 NIV)

Describe how you most often hear the Lord speaking to you. What can you improve in your prayer pattern to be more aware of Him speaking to your heart? Are you listening intently for His response?

7

WHY ME?

I can't say that this journey has been a constant trek forward. It's been more of a constant dance of two steps forward and one step back.

I've had <u>a lot</u> of "why me" questions, especially in the beginning. As my world had been turned upside down, I watched others enjoying perfection and fell into a pit of bitter jealousy:

Why is this happening to me? I follow Jesus. I obey God's commands. I don't deserve this. I don't need a trial to find Jesus; I already have Him in my life. Why doesn't this happen to my (relative, coworker, neighbor) who needs to find God in a dark valley? Everything works out perfectly for them, but I get this. And my baby has to suffer! It's not fair! Doesn't God promise good things to those who love Him? He's giving my (relative, coworker, neighbor) such an easy street, and He's ruining my life and my child's life with this! Why doesn't He answer my pleading for relief? Why is He letting this happen to me and to my baby?

My mother played Socrates to help me overcome the "why me?" with an opposing question: why not me? God knew I would learn to seek His will, learn to accept His peace, and learn to display His grace in this trial. So why wouldn't He use me? Why wouldn't He choose me?

Maybe God chose you to carry your burden because He trusts you to use it for His glory. He knows He can work through you to accomplish extraordinary things.

Why did God choose Mary to mother His Son? Because she "found favor with God." I imagine teenage Mary wasn't full of complete joy and peace when the angel Gabriel informed her that she would give birth to the Son of the Creator. She must have had some feelings of confusion and worry, even anger and dismay. But she accepted and embraced the difficult times ahead of her—because God chose her: "I am the Lord's servant. Let it be to me as you have said."

God's divine plan is so much bigger than we can imagine, and even though we don't understand it now, He does. He knew what He was doing when He chose you to carry your burdens, so trust Him, because He wants to use you.

Refresh yourself in God's Word; read Luke 1:26–38. Although none of us are entrusted with such a noble purpose as Mary was, draw a mental parallel between your commission and hers.

_____

_____

_____

_____

_____

_____

_____

_____

_____

8

WHAT IF I'M JUST NOT ENOUGH?

Another backward step on the journey on which God had placed me was this: in preparing for the scenario in which Joelle would have DiGeorge syndrome, my fears and selfishness would arise.

What if I don't love this baby enough? What if my heart just isn't big enough to give this child the love she needs? What if I don't connect with her? What if the stress of caring for a disabled child is too great, and I end up resenting my life? What if I'm just not enough? I must be a selfish monster! But my fears are real.

As the day of delivery neared, I had to come to terms with preparing Joelle's nursery. I had put it off until the end because I didn't have the excitement about welcoming a perfectly healthy new baby like other moms had the joy of experiencing. I was worried. I was sad. How could I create a happy space for a baby when I was sad for her and sad for myself? Regardless, this baby was coming, whether I was emotionally and spiritually ready or not, so I'd better be physically organized.

Roll out the paint. Assemble the crib. Hang the curtains. Organize the changing table. Just do the one next thing ... and gradually ... two steps forward.

Somehow the motherly task of physically readying the nursery gave me the motherly excitement and love that I was missing. I was now ready for this baby to get here. I just wanted to sit in that new chair and rock her in that beautiful, glowing room. I wanted to meet her. I wanted to care for her. I wanted to hold her and love her.

Lord, I'm ready for this.

Feelings of being ill-equipped to face a hardship you have no experience in is completely normal. I wasn't a selfish monster because of my fears, and if you are feeling anything similar in your situation, neither are you. *But God does not want us to let those fears take over or allow selfishness any space in our hearts.*

Sometimes the physical process of doing what should be done puts our minds and hearts in the right place. We have to go through the physical steps and acts, and naturally, ours hearts fall in line. Of course, this is not accomplished without prayer.

If you are frozen by, stuck in, or wrestling fear, try doing the one next thing to step through that fear while praying for the strength to overcome it. God is bigger than all fear. God is love. Love is not selfish. God answers prayer; fear will subside, and love will grow.

> Such love has no fear, because perfect love expels all fear. If we are afraid, it is for fear of punishment, and this shows that we have not experienced His perfect love.
> (1 John 4:18 NLT)

Record your fears and the next physical steps you need to take in the process you are facing. Honestly tell God about those fears and ask Him to eliminate them while you take the next physical step in your journey.

_____

_____

_____

_____

_____

_____

MOLLY HANKEY

9

GOD GIVES US PEOPLE

Mary had Elizabeth. Ruth had Naomi. Silas had Paul. I had Amy.

The initial email that we sent to our family and friends asking for prayer detailed the preliminary heart defect diagnosis we received from the twenty-two-week ultrasound. That email was forwarded again and again and landed in Amy's inbox. Disbelieving it was real at first, she traced and investigated sources to validate it. Why did she go to so much trouble for one of those mass forwards that we would normally skim over, say a quick prayer about, and then delete? Because her son had the same rare heart defect as we were told Joelle would have.

Amy reached out to me through email, introducing her family and sharing some of their story. She selflessly made herself available to me, a total stranger, to help me in my time of need. She was completing her full circle. Just a few years before, Amy had been in my shoes and had leaned on someone else who had been through a similar situation. She survived the storm, gained wisdom, and was now ready to pass it on—*to me*.

We developed a friendship through email over the next few months. She was local, and her son had been treated by the same hospital and specialist group that we were using. It was fantastic to be able to have questions answered about doctors, processes, logistics, and more. But for some introverted reason, I was reserved about actually meeting with her face-to-face.

One day close to the end of my pregnancy, Amy emailed me from her work email address, which had a familiar domain. I put two and two together and realized she worked for an agency that shared my office building, and I had unknowingly walked past her office door a hundred times! I was overwhelmed with astonishment! I took this as a God-sign and let go of my inhibitions about meeting her.

As I walked into her office the next day and told her who I was, we both turned into teary messes and shared one of the warmest embraces of my life. She showed me pictures of her son, which filled me with hope for Joelle. And when she prayed with me, right there in her office, I knew we would be forever connected.

Amy continued to offer encouragement and support through Joelle's birth and hospitalization. She was the only one who completely understood the extent of pain and detail of difficulty I was having as a brand-new mom of a "heart baby." She opened up her heart and relived her own pain in order to help me through mine. I believe we both experienced emotional healing. Only God could have facilitated healing our hearts like this.

God places people in our lives during times of uncertainty and hardship who serve as guides, mentors, and shoulders to lean on. These people are relatable to us because they have been through similar circumstances. Because of that, they have greater wisdom than we do. When we are swimming in an ocean of emotion and are having trouble seeing the light, God sends us blessings in the form of people.

Like Ruth sought from Naomi, seek comfort, wisdom, and guidance from those He's placed in your life who have been through what you are going through. Be willing to listen to advice from experienced, wise counsel. Thank the Lord for placing people in your life who have seen and overcome the same hardships you are facing.

> And she replied, "All you say I will do."
> (Ruth 3:5 ESV)

Has God blessed you with anyone in your life who has experienced what you are going through? Can you look to them for guidance, wisdom, and an understanding shoulder to lean on? God designed us to live in community, not guarded isolation, so lean into these people He's given you. List your person or people below. If you're already connected, how have they helped you so far? If you haven't tapped into their insight, will you come together with them to take advantage of the gift God's given?

_____

_____

_____

_____

_____

_____

_____

_____

_____

_____

_____

_____

_____

_____

10

SOURCE OF STRENGTH

Joelle's delivery was not smooth or easy. It followed no birth plan I had in mind. Thankfully, it took place in a first-rate hospital, or she and I both would be long gone.

After nineteen hours of laborious torture, nine-pound-six-ounces, twenty-two-inch Joelle said goodbye to her cozy nine-month home and took her first breath of air.

The doctor held her up for me to look at, and then she was immediately conveyed to the other side of the room to be examined, hooked up to monitors, and have an IV line placed. There were more than ten doctors, nurses, and spectator interns bustling around. It was the opposite of peaceful. Jim was flitting back and forth between my side as I was being cared for and watching Joelle as instruments and monitors whirled around her little body. His words were few, as the chaos rendered him wide-eyed and emotional.

Drugs were kicking in, and I fell into a haze as pain finally lessened and sleep became a possibility. Floating on the edge of dreamland, I became oddly and uncomfortably fixated on my bewildering perception that Joelle looked exactly like my dad. Then a sharp, awakening voice, "Give her a kiss, Mom," prompted a masked woman in green scrubs, and she tilted Joelle's little face down to my lips. One kiss, and she was whisked away to the NICU.

The next seven hours flew by as I was transferred from room to room, checked continuously by nurses and visited by one specialist or consultant after another. Finally, the night shift came on, and my room got quiet. Out of my mind with exhaustion, I ached for sleep and had just closed my eyes when my father encouraged me to go see Joelle in the NICU. I told him I'd go as soon as I woke up. "You really ought to go *now*," he urged, with more words emanating from his eyes than his mouth. Through the cracks of my ten-pound eyelids, I saw his face and understood. I had better go see her now, while I can, just in case the worst happens.

God, I need Your divine energy and strength, because I am out.

He gave me what I needed. The nurse readied my IV bags and monitors. My mother groomed me to look presentable. I still had little feeling in my legs, so Jim hoisted me into the wheelchair and pushed me toward the NICU. On the way there, my motherly hormones started surging. I became overly anxious and desperately impatient on the trek to where my baby waited for me. Suddenly irritated at the traveling distance between the maternity ward and NICU, I barked at Jim, "Can't you push this thing any faster?"

At long last, we entered the NICU vestibule. The mandatory two-minute handwashing with iodine soap and specialized fingernail scrubbers seemed to last an hour. I hurriedly fumbled through donning the special NICU gown; tying a simple bow seemed impossible. *I just want to see my baby!*

Finally, we went in. Jim took me through a maze of bassinets and incubators filled with micro, premature infants no larger than my hand. But there in the back of the room lay my big, beautiful, peacefully sleeping, newborn baby girl.

The bonding that takes place between a mother and her baby at birth, through skin-to-skin contact, is real. As soon as I touched her buttery skin, let her tiny fingers wrap around mine, and stroked her silky baby hair, all of my motherly senses awakened, and I knew I would be hers forever. The tears flowed, and the love abounded so much my heart physically hurt.

And I had been worried I wouldn't love this baby enough ...

God will give you the strength to do what He has created you to do. His timing may seem impossible on all human levels. His call may seem too burdensome. You may feel like you have nothing left ... but *He* does.

His strength is unceasing and will renew you—body, mind and soul. His plan will prevail in your life.

> My flesh and my heart may fail, but God is the strength
> of my heart and my portion forever.
> (Psalm 73:26 NIV)

Are you exhausted? Discouraged? Helpless? Tell God how finished you are. Empty out all the emotion tucked in every crevice of your heart. Then ask Him for His almighty strength. Listen for His clear voice. He'll fill you with His wisdom and give you His strength to do what He's created you to do. Take some quiet time now to connect with our ultimate source of strength in prayer.

_____

_____

_____

_____

_____

_____

_____

_____

_____

_____

_____

11

TRANSFORMING THANKSGIVING

Timely and divinely designed, I was discharged from the maternity ward on Thanksgiving Day. Consequentially, that became the most memorable Thanksgiving of my life as well as the most meaningful. Our home being an hour away from the hospital was less than convenient, since Joelle remained hospitalized indefinitely. How on earth would we manage this? Enter the Ronald McDonald House.

The RMH provided us a beautiful, free home right across the street from the hospital. Free home-cooked meals, a fully stocked pantry for anything else we might want to eat, and all the luxuries and comforts of home while we were physically drained and emotionally devastated. When your baby is in the NICU and you live an hour away, life is not easy. RMH made it easier.

An added and unexpected bonus was the camaraderie we formed with other families with hospitalized children. Walking with others through their struggles refocused my mind when I was chest deep in my own. While I was receiving so much from this house, friending others helped me to give at the same time. There's a great mystery of emotional healing when one gives through their pain.

The slogan for our local RMH is "the house that love built." There is truly a palpable love that hangs in the air of that house and I assume any other RMH. It emanates from the host of volunteers and staff that give their all to take care of hurting families. We can't say enough good things about RMH. We are eternally thankful for this organization, the donors who support it, and the people who work to make it amazing.

Your love for one another will prove to the world that you
are my disciples. (John 13:35 NLT)

Christians form the body of Christ; the body has many parts that
perform different functions. God has gifted each of us with a spiritual
specialty that we are to use in serving and loving others. Sometimes we
are the giver, sometimes we are the receiver, and sometimes we are both
at the same time.

Being the receiver develops in us a deeper level of thanksgiving that
can transform us into better and more cognizant givers. Had I not had
this struggle in my life, I wouldn't have grown in maturity of servanthood.

Receive the love from the body of Christ. Let the hands of Christ serve
you in your time of need. Let the ears listen to your troubles, let the arms
shoulder your cries, and let the voice pray with you.

Have you allowed the body of Christ to serve you in your need? How
has your appreciation of this transformed your heart for serving others?
Have you experienced emotional healing through serving?

_____

_____

_____

_____

_____

_____

_____

_____

12

DEEPEST GRATITUDE

Joelle's official cardiology diagnosis is tetralogy of Fallot, with pulmonary atresia. I'll spare you the extensive definition but will say there were seven abnormalities in her heart and blood vessels, and she would not survive even one month without corrective surgery. She would have her first open-heart surgery at one week old. We met with her surgeon on Black Friday to discuss it and sign the forms.

As I was still recovering from a problematic delivery, Jim pushed me in a wheelchair across the whole hospital from the state-of-the-art NICU to the surgeon's office in an old dusky hallway. As we entered the room, I couldn't help but notice the surgeon's stature. He was a solid, husky fellow with hands like bear paws. *How can these hands manipulate such tiny organs and surgical instruments and operate on such delicate tissues?* By God-given talent, I would come to find out.

This is a highly renowned pediatric cardiothoracic surgeon, with now more than three decades of experience. He has outstanding surgical outcomes, and we are incredibly fortunate to have him on Joelle's team. I thank the Lord for him and his medical team of doctors and nurses who are using their God-given skills to keep Joelle's heart pumping.

He discussed the corrective approaches he would take to attempt to normalize Joelle's heart. He spoke of a bypass machine and Gortex patches … a five-hour surgery, and that a newborn's heart is the size of a walnut. He explained collateral arteries, an overriding aorta, septal defects, and blood-oxygen levels. At that moment, just four days after meeting our daughter, my mind strained to comprehend.

What I remember as clear as day was how he spoke of implanting a new pulmonary valve. I asked what it was made of, thinking it would be a porcine or bovine valve, as I had heard about adults receiving valves from pigs and cows. He replied that because a newborn's heart is so small, the valves used must be suitably sized donor valves from other human newborns … cadavers.

In a sorrowful, horrendous realization that my baby would benefit from another's loss of life, I held back my urge to vomit as I let that information sink in. As much as I was dealing with—facing my one-week-old surviving open-heart surgery, still wondering if she had a genetic disorder, and dealing with my own physically debilitating pain from delivery—it was nowhere near as heavy as other parents' grief who had lost their babies.

These selfless and generous parents, while drowning in their loss and heartache, donated their beautiful angels' organs to help other children like mine. I have always been an organ donor myself, as listed on my driver's license since I was sixteen, but that is an entirely different level of decision than choosing to hand over your deceased infant's body for organ harvesting.

To this day, I wish I could meet the parents of the child who helped my daughter live. I would thank them with the most sincere gratitude. I pray they know how thankful we are for their thoughtfulness and mindfulness during their adversity.

As passing years have distanced me from the acute pain of the crisis, I have been able to reflect and identify the perfect plan God had laid out. No, the journey isn't over, and I know there's more pain ahead, but I can see the pits behind us that God brought my family through. I can see how He constructed a perfectly orchestrated web of people and events that He used to sustain my daughter's life. Words cannot express how entirely thankful I am … now.

When I was in a whirlwind of despair and unpredictable emotion, I wasn't thinking about God's prearranged assembly of individuals and actions that would affect the outcome of our situation. If I had been able

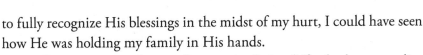

to fully recognize His blessings in the midst of my hurt, I could have seen how He was holding my family in His hands.

Perhaps you are in the pit of your pain. It *is* a difficult place to realize the blessings God's given you. But He *has* blessed you, He *does* love you, and He *will* deliver you if you hold onto to Him. Keep following Him, and eventually you will come to a place of deepest gratitude.

> I will come and proclaim your mighty acts, O Sovereign
> Lord; I will proclaim your righteousness, yours alone ...
> Though you have made me see troubles, many and bitter,
> you will restore my life again. (Psalm 71:16, 20 NIV)

If you haven't identified the web of people that God has used and is using in your life to sustain you in your trial, acknowledge those blessings now.

_____

_____

_____

_____

_____

_____

_____

_____

_____

_____

13

INADEQUATE WORDS

One week old. Surgery day. We arrived at the hospital around 5:30 a.m. to hold Joelle and breathe her in. I seesawed between calm peace and heart-gripping fear.

What if she doesn't make it? What if this is the last time I hold my baby?

Jim realized we hadn't yet taken a family picture of our new family of three. We hadn't the opportunity for those sweet first-day photos on the day Joelle was born. This might be the only chance we had to pose for a picture with our baby girl still breathing. The nurse took the camera, and we did our best to smile through our worry. It wasn't pretty but illustrated the moment. We ended up using that picture on our Christmas card.

The time came for Joelle to be taken to the operating room. The most difficult moment had arrived. We sat in her room, helpless as we watched her in her bassinet being wheeled away. Words cannot describe the deep, painful, sorrowful fear that I felt at the possibility I would not see my baby alive again. The seesaw levered, and calm peace fled. Aching fear was my single emotion remaining.

"Please, God" were the only words my brain could conjure, and I prayed them over and over and over for the next few hours. I went to the chapel and prayed. I went outside and prayed. I went to the cafeteria and prayed. And then I ran out of prayers. I sat in the waiting room, drained. Sleep evaded me, even though my eyes were so heavy. I became irritable as I sat helpless, listening to the trivial conversations of strangers.

Time started passing even more slowly as I became more restless and worrisome. Then, in the middle of the fourth hour, a rainbow stepped through the clouds. The social worker who had been handling our case found us in the waiting room and delivered a double dose of delight:

"The surgery has progressed well. The surgeon was able to perform even more correction than originally hoped for. Joelle is off the bypass machine, and her heart is beating by itself." *Air into my lungs.*

"Also, genetic testing results have come back, and Joelle does *not* have DiGeorge syndrome." *Thank You, God!*

Jesus, I don't even have the words to thank You. You have brought us through storm and fire and have now blessed us so completely! Words are inadequate ...

When words don't come close to describing your heart, whether it be drowning with sorrow or bursting with thanksgiving, just *be* with God in prayer. When your mind is too fatigued to form words, just rest in God's presence. Meditate on His brilliant, radiant grace. Visually place yourself at His feet, at His throne. Physically kneel before Him. Actually raise up your hands in praise or in need.

Our Lord God knows your heart, your needs, and your love for Him. Sometimes prayer is simply offering your heart to Him so He can unload it and fill it with His peace.

Take some time to "Be still, and know that I am God!" (Psalm 46:10a NIV). No words, just be.

> You have searched me Lord, and You know me ... Before
> a word is on my tongue, You, Lord, know it completely.
> (Psalm 139:1, 4 NIV)

14

BROKEN

Simply grateful that Joelle was coming through surgery alive, I had forgotten about the healing road she had ahead.

We had met with our social worker before Joelle's birth and had seen the pediatric ICU where she would be cared for post-surgery. We had been shown the steps of care so we knew what to expect: a mess of wires, tubes, machines, and a tin foil oxygen tent placed over her head. What I wasn't prepared to handle was the five-inch-long, bright red incision wound that marred her little chest like an ugly war souvenir. Of course I knew it was coming; open-heart surgery involves cutting through the sternum. But surveying the aftermath gave me the full mental visualization of what happened to my baby's little body in that operating room. Additionally, she was blown up like a balloon with the extra fluid her body was retaining. Her petite face was now puffed up and distorted with the ventilator and feeding tubes taped to her mouth and nose. She was nearly unrecognizable.

Joelle's post-surgery nurses were cardiac specialists, handpicked and trained by the surgeon. They worked solely on Joelle for the first twenty-four critical hours after surgery and were the busiest nurses in the PICU. They packed Joelle with ice packs as her body temperature rocketed to 105. They monitored and reacted to three different beeping machines, administered medications into IVs, weighed every wet diaper, and taught me about everything that was connected to and inserted in my child. They were warrior nurses.

Others hovering over Joelle included the cardiology physician's assistant, intensive specialist, nurse practitioner, and resident doctor. There was no shortage of attention, intelligence, or knowledge.

Even with the preparation we received with the social worker, the knowledge of Joelle's surgery going so well, and watching the extensive staff giving her the highest-rated care, the whole scene was extremely difficult to handle.

As Joelle's tiny wrists and ankles were tethered down to prevent her from knocking loose any of her tubes and wires, my hands were tied in taking away her pain, which is all I longed to do. I couldn't hold her, help her, or heal her. My heart was more broken than hers.

There's a cliché I'm sure you've heard before, "let go and let God," meaning we should let go of troubles and let God handle them for us. Personally, I find that saying obnoxiously irritating because it is *much* easier said than done, until we are at that point of complete helplessness. Then we have no choice but to let go of our false sense of control. We do have the choice to let God give us peace in our distress while He handles the situation that He's always been in control of.

Jochebed, desperate to save her baby from a brutal drowning by the hand of the Egyptians, did all she could do to save her baby from death. With no means left to hide her son, she put her three-month-old baby in a basket, in a river, and let go (Exodus 2:1–10). She was at the point of complete helplessness. With no other choice, she let God take complete control. Of course, this was all part of God's amazing plan, and things turned out well in the end for Jochebed and her baby, Moses.

We have no idea how our circumstances will end, but we can be certain that our stories are also part of God's amazing plan. Remember that when you are broken, at the point of complete helplessness, and you are forced to let go; let God give you peace.

Are you completely broken? Helpless? Record your thoughts and prayer as you let go and let God give you peace:

15

THE WAVES KEEP CRASHING

In reality, Joelle's recovery from that first surgery was speedy. It took her only twelve days post-surgery to recover enough for discharge. Walking through that time was a different story. Time seemed to pass at snail speed. Spending sixteen hours a day in an ICU drives one a little batty. I felt imprisoned, like we were being held captive. I kept having an irrational urge to rip off Joelle's tubes and wires, pick her up, and escape.

Finally, discharge day came, but it wasn't as joyous as I was expecting. It was a Saturday morning when a doctor we hadn't met before came into the room. "Your daughter is ready to be discharged, but she'll need to go home on supplemental oxygen." His delivery of the news was abrupt and harsh, and I was caught completely off guard.

What? In shock, throat tight, tears welling, mind racing … *This was not part of the plan. No one told me about this possibility before. Can't she stay until she's better? Why isn't she better? Will she get better? I don't know how to care for a baby on oxygen! I don't even know how to care for a normal baby yet!*

The doctor could not give us any guesses as to how long Joelle might need the oxygen, just an explanation of why. A normal blood-oxygen level is 99–100 percent. Joelle's was 84 percent with the additional oxygen and only 77 percent without it. She needed extra to mitigate the risk of damage to her brain and body.

So discharge arrangements were made. We were given education on oxygen cylinder tanks, five different medications, incision-wound care, and how to pick up a baby with a wired-together sternum. The nurse unhooked Joelle from her monitors and removed the last of her IV ports. We figured out how to put baby clothes on her, around an oxygen tube and tank. We dressed her in a special take-home outfit and strapped her into the brand-new infant carrier. It felt like a surreal dream, walking out of the hospital with a baby in tow. *And we weren't sure if we were capable of handling it all.* Instead of a jubilant departure, it was a frighteningly nervous one.

> Peter got down out of the boat, walked on the water and came toward Jesus. But when he saw the wind, he was afraid and, beginning to sink, cried out, "Lord, save me!" Immediately Jesus reached out his hand and caught him. "You of little faith," he said, "why did you doubt?" (Matthew 14:29–31 NIV)

It isn't fun getting pummeled by waves. Just when you think you've found your footing, another one knocks you sideways. You find yourself flailing, searching for solid ground. It sounds so simple, yet it's so humanly difficult to do—keep your eyes on Jesus and walk above the waves. I didn't do that in my situation, but I hope you will in yours. When you become apprehensive and start to sink, look to Jesus, who will immediately catch you, just as He did with Peter.

Are you sinking or are your eyes fixed on Jesus?

_____

_____

_____

_____

_____

_____

_____

16

FORGETFULLY ANGRY

Weeks and months went by, and how I longed to see my baby's beautiful face without that fat, ugly, plastic oxygen tube veiling her. I hadn't seen her plain face since she was one week old, the morning before her surgery.

Beyond the appearance of the tube, the difficulties of the physical logistics were endless. Sometimes the tube would get caught on a doorknob or table corner as I carried her by it, and it would jerk her head abruptly. Sometimes it would get pulled tightly across her face and distort her nose. Sometimes she would rub her nose with her little baby fist, and I wouldn't notice for a few minutes that the nasal prongs had popped out and migrated up to her eyebrows. I felt like an unfit mother when any of that happened, especially when other people were the first to notice and brought it to my attention.

Joelle sported plastic stickers on the sides of her face to hold the tube in place. They collected dust, dirt, and fuzz and made her pretty little baby face appear dirty and damaged. When it was time to change them, they left big red marks on her skin and got stuck in her baby peach fuzz hair. I can only imagine how painful that was for her delicate infant skin.

These are just a few examples; there were many more issues to contend with. The tube had become my nemesis, and I *hated* It.

At seven months old, Joelle underwent an extensive sedated echocardiogram to assess her heart's growth and fitness. She had monthly cardiology appointments up until this time, where her blood-oxygen level showed no improvement. I was hopeful that the doctor would see some sort of progress in this extensive examination so we could ditch "the tube".

Instead, he came out of the exam room with *that look* on his face, deflating our optimism. He said Joelle might *always* need supplemental oxygen and tried his best to help us not be afraid of that.

Nonetheless, his attempts didn't help my anxiety-ridden self. Furthermore, he requested that Joelle undergo a more invasive heart catheterization to explore parts of her heart unable to be seen with an echocardiogram. New angst, depression, and anger set in to my soul.

I was acting like an Israelite in the desert, forgetting that God had just delivered my family from Egypt through the Red Sea, and then complaining angrily, thinking God had brought us into the desert to die. I forgot what God had done for us and for Joelle. I lost faith that He would deliver us in His time and His way.

God's plans are different from ours. His timing is different from ours. He always has a reason, a lesson, a purpose in what He gives us. Our anger doesn't do anything but separate us from Him, the one we need the most to help us through our trials. The closer we get to Him, the faster we learn the lesson, the faster our hearts will grow, which in turn lightens our burdens.

Please don't be an Israelite like I was. God is the Creator of the universe. He set this Earth into motion. He made us, He loves us, and He sacrificed His Son to save us. We are unwise to be angry with Him. Instead, we should trust His time and His means in deliverance.

> But those who trust in the Lord will find new strength.
> They will soar high on wings like Eagles. They will run
> and not grow weary. They will walk and not faint.
> (Isaiah 40:31 NLT)

Are you angry with God? If so, is it helping you or is it further damaging your heart?

_____

_____

_____

_____

Have you forgotten the good things He has done for you? Will you trust Him to deliver you from your heartache?

_____

_____

_____

_____

_____

_____

_____

_____

_____

_____

_____

_____

_____

17

DIAMONDS OUT OF DUST

With no more hope and in a valley of darkness, I *finally* gave it all to God—*every* last bit of anger and worry that I had been clutching so tightly to for so long. I had of course been praying all along about the oxygen issue and even for Jesus to fully heal Joelle's heart. But it wasn't until now, when I had hit my rock bottom—where I had lost all hope that my child would ever be physically *normal*—that I released *everything* to God. I gave Him my burden because I couldn't carry it anymore.

Subsequently, my prayers changed because my heart changed. I prayed for Him to teach me how to walk through the ups and downs of life with a disabled child. I prayed for peace in my heart.

And God gave me a gift. He taught me how to use Joelle's condition to talk to people about Him. It was then that I really began to embrace her special needs. Instead of ignoring strangers' stares at my tube-laden baby, I'd strike up conversations with them about God's grace and how He had blessed us with Joelle.

Joelle's personality made it easier to talk to people about her. She was a happy, bubbly baby. As soon as she learned how to smile and wave, she did so not just to friends and family but also to random strangers in public. It opened up opportunities to share God's miracles with others. For what was lacking in Joelle's good health, God had overcompensated with a radiant personality. Being able to share His love with others through my child was a shining diamond that I never expected.

So often, we won't fully hand things over to God until we have hit rock bottom. It is so hard to stop wrestling the balance of worry and hope until there is no hope left and worries develop into reality. Rock bottom is the place where we fully accept that reality and fully realize we can't do anything about it. God takes the dust we make from hitting rock bottom and transforms it into shiny, gleaming diamonds.

Look at Job. He was reduced to nothing—far worse than anything most any other human has ever experienced. In my human mind, he had every right to bitterness and complaints, which is what he held onto for a long time. He held that anger and despair so tightly and so self-righteously until he got scolded—by God Himself. That's when Job finally hit his own rock bottom. Only after this, God turned things around for Job and created diamonds in his life again.

> "Surely I spoke of things I did not understand, things too wonderful for me to know … Therefore I despise myself and repent in dust and ashes." … The Lord made him prosperous again and gave him twice as much as he had before … The Lord blessed the latter part of Job's life more than the first. (Job 42:3, 6, 10, 12 NIV)

Describe your rock bottom. Have you yet seen the diamonds God has made with your dust?

_____

_____

_____

_____

_____

_____

_____

18

HIS PERFECT TIMING

As Joelle got older and started crawling, the oxygen became more of a tether and obstruction than just a cumbersome, ugly discontentment. Her body or legs would get wrapped up in the tube, or she wouldn't be able to go where she wanted because her tube wasn't long enough. I wondered how it would impact her learning to walk.

When she was nine months old, I started praying about the oxygen again, that if it could fit into His will, Jesus would put His healing hand on Joelle. I prayed from the depth of my soul that He would alleviate her need for the oxygen before she learned to walk. It wasn't a prayer derived from my hatred of "the tube" or the fact that it made my child abnormal. It stemmed rather from a logistical need; I knew that God would provide a way for Joelle to walk regardless, but it would be so much easier for her if she wasn't tethered to an oxygen tank. My heart broke for her, imagining her toddling, not being able to roam free, being tied like a dog on a leash. *So I didn't give this prayer a rest.*

At thirteen months old, we went to her monthly cardiology appointment, one week before Christmas. The doctor did the routine blood-oxygen level check, comparing the numbers with her oxygen on and then without it. Joelle's blood oxygen level was 89 percent on the supplemental oxygen and 89 percent off of it. He checked it again. And one more time to be sure. As I watched this unfold, I sat speechless, in shock and disbelief.

Our miracle was realized. Joelle's heart and vessels had somehow come to a point of healing, where the extra oxygen being given to her didn't make a difference in her blood-oxygen level. So she didn't need it anymore. Jesus had healed Joelle's body in a way that modern medicine and surgery couldn't. The doctor said the words I had been hoping to hear for an entire year: "No more oxygen!"

Months before, I had dreamed of the day Joelle would be tube-free. I imagined a big celebration, a grand announcement, a bonfire to burn the tubes and the tattered oxygen tank carrying case. When the time finally came to remove Joelle's accessories, however, God hushed me with a quiet peace. I will always remember that still moment, taking the tube and the stickers off of her face, turning off the oxygen supply, and looking at her sitting in her crib, unattached to anything. It was surreal, and I had to wrap my brain around it. It wasn't the moment of booming triumph I had imagined but was a peaceful culmination of a journey.

I carried Joelle, unattached to anything, all over the house, to rooms and corners she couldn't reach before because her tube wasn't long enough. And then I said, "Well, that's that," and that was the extent of my celebration. The absence of the oxygen tube didn't seem as big of a deal to me as I thought it would be.

Of course, I was remarkably thankful and elated, for God had positively answered my prayer and changed my daughter's life; what an advantage for her to be able to move freely without hindrance! But the complete peace the Lord gave me erased all disparity and bitterness I had felt before; I no longer felt the need for a grandiose commemoration.

One week later, in God's perfect timing, Joelle took her very first steps—on Christmas Day. What a Christmas present that was!

I am not formally educated on prayer. I don't have the seven keys to prayer, the plan for prayer, powerful prayers for peace, or any other elevated, educated knowledge other than what I have read in God's Good Book and what I have seen modeled by more mature Christians than myself.

But I do have experience in prayer. I have been praying my entire life and have prayed about many different things.

I've learned that we are to pray in accordance with God's will and timing, while aligning our hearts with His. Of course God doesn't give us everything we ask for, right when we want it. He parents us just like we parent our children. I waited thirteen months for God to say yes about healing Joelle's heart to the point where she would not need supplemental oxygen. I also knew that this might not be in His will for her life. By praying for His will to be completed and trusting in His timing, He quieted my heart with His peace about either outcome.

Pray for miracles, but pray in accordance with God's will. If your initial request doesn't fit His plan, He will transform your hurting heart and cover you with His peace that passes understanding. His promise in that stands true forever.

> He heals the brokenhearted and binds up their wounds.
> (Psalm 147:3 NIV)

Are you praying to align your heart and your desires with God's plan? Do you trust His Will and timing?

_____

_____

_____

_____

_____

_____

_____

_____

_____

19

UNFATHOMABLE MIRACLE

The average person's blood-oxygen level is 98–100 percent. Joelle had survived her first year at numbers between 74 and 89 percent. This was concerning, especially considering she was a developing child. She did exhibit low muscle tone but was still able to do what she needed to do. She was meeting all the general milestones mentally and physically, but we were worried about how the low level of oxygen in her body would affect her brain and muscle development over the long term. So of course we lifted this in prayer to The Healer … *and He put icing on our cake.*

At Joelle's next cardiology appointment in January, one month after she came off the supplemental oxygen, her blood-oxygen level had improved *remarkably* and without reason—to 96 percent! I looked at the doctor, dumbfounded, with my jaw on the floor. "It's a miracle!"

And he was quick to agree. He said, "I've been doing this long enough that I know things happen like this that I can't explain medically, and I believe that God has definitely helped her along here." God is good all the time, but oh how He piled on the goodness that day!

I have prayed to God for things in my life and the lives of others', and He has answered, "No." This is one of the times I got a yes.

Don't be afraid to pray for a divine miracle. If you don't ask, you might miss the blessing. If you do ask and the answer is no, then pray for wisdom to understand why and peace that surpasses your understanding of the situation. Always pray to align your heart with God's will.

The Bible lays out one event after another showcasing God's amazing miracles. He rescues one person after another, from Genesis through Revelation. These were people of faith and prayer, calling on God and Jesus to see them through hardships and danger and asking for miracles to change their lives. These people were just like us. Furthermore, God is the same as He was then. He performs amazing, life-changing, scientifically unexplainable miracles *every day*. If you pray earnestly, consistently, and humbly, you might get a yes.

> He performs wonders that cannot be fathomed, miracles that cannot be counted. (Job 5:9 NIV)

> Jesus Christ is the same yesterday and today and forever. (Hebrews 13:8 NIV)

What is your request for a seemingly impossible, unfathomable miracle? How will you pray about it?

_____

_____

_____

_____

_____

_____

_____

20

LOVE IS

Joelle was now fourteen months old. The next nine months were bliss, where Jim and I enjoyed parenting a nearly "normal" child. We had no more oxygen tanks or tubes to deal with. Joelle was growing better and faster than she ever had because of her increased blood-oxygen level. She was gaining a lot of muscle strength and tone. It was fantastic. Our stress levels had come down to easily manageable, which was *much* better for our marriage.

The first year of a baby's life is one of the most stressful seasons a couple will experience together—even if the baby is perfectly healthy! Add in medical equipment, feeding aversions, slow growth, four different doctors' appointments per month, extensive medical bills, and a new mom with anxiety and depression issues, and you have a recipe for some marital strife.

Right now I want to speak specifically to those of you who are married. I certainly am not a relationship expert or marriage counselor, but I do have life experience in it, and my marriage has survived several courses of seriously rocky terrain. How?

Jim and I have always honored the truth that God should be the center of a marriage. God comes first. Period. As you each grow closer to God, you will grow closer to each other. We have seen both sides of that coin: growing closer and straying further. And we've sat right on the rounded edge of that coin too, stuck in the rut, going nowhere. Our marriage is only truly cohesive, fulfilling, and happy when we are both growing closer to Jesus.

The second truth that we had been taught but was harder for me to put into practice at that time is that spouses need to put each other's needs first; God-centered marriage relationships should take priority over parent-child relationships. That was harder for me than Jim. In fact, it was hard for me to even swallow; I didn't fully agree with it. Created as a nurturing mother, I naturally put the needs of my child over my own, so why wouldn't I put the needs of my child over the needs of my husband? And why didn't Jim understand why I thought that way?

It took me the whole first year of parenthood to just understand the concept of putting my marriage first while meeting the physical, mental, and emotional needs of our child. Learning the art and science of properly balancing and ordering marriage and parenthood is an ongoing experience that continuously evolves. It takes practice and regular evaluation, like anything else you work at.

I had to learn not to emotionally abandon my husband while I was preoccupied with meeting the needs of our child. Jim had to learn patience with me and to be more understanding of how I was wired. We are still learning to this day.

I could probably write a book on this topic alone, not because I have it mastered but because I have messed it up many, many times. It is a hard thing to grasp and become proficient at in today's society, especially for women. It definitely has been difficult for me. Looking back at this particular time in our lives, I have to give props to my husband, who put up with an extensive amount of unpleasantness from me while we were both navigating the new world of parenting a special needs child.

The bottom line: a happy parental relationship equals a happy child. Children can see and feel strain in the relationships surrounding them. Even as babies, they are far more intuitive than we sometimes give them credit for. Ill feelings and attitudes toward your partner are picked up on by your children, which has the potential to render them emotionally insecure and unbalanced. Again, I speak this from experience in observing my own children in the rocky stretches of my own marriage.

The best gift you can give your child is to honor, respect, and love your spouse, first. Make sure that relationship is strong, so you can both be stronger together for your child. It is a continuous work in progress.

We see the love passage from 1 Corinthians so often; it's almost overused in Christian literature, art, media, and so on, to the point where it doesn't penetrate our hearts. We're calloused to it. We skim over it, we know it, we get it. But ... are we living it out with our spouses? Take some time to ponder every individual word in this passage. Ask yourself if you are really applying it to your marriage, and remember that we all have room for improvement.

> Love is patient and kind; love does not envy or boast; it is not arrogant or rude. It does not insist on its own way; it is not irritable or resentful; it does not rejoice at wrongdoing, but rejoices with the truth. Love bears all things, believes all things, hopes all things, endures all things. (1 Corinthians 13:4–7 ESV)

_____

_____

_____

_____

_____

_____

_____

_____

_____

_____

21

CHANGING SEASONS

We had been told that Joelle's next corrective open-heart surgery would need to take place when she was approximately two years old, so that was looming in the back of our minds during those blissful nine months. Eventually, that next surgery reared its ugly head.

Joelle needed a new pulmonary valve—the valve that connects the heart to the arteries that take the blood to the lungs. Her cadaver valve she received at birth was failing, as it was expected to at her age.

October 25—twenty-three months old. This surgery was textbook routine, and she was only supposed to be in the hospital for a week. That didn't happen. Joelle suffered some complications during her surgery. She had a reprofusion injury, where too much blood from her pulmonary arteries entered her lungs too fast. Her lungs were filled with blood and fluid. She couldn't breathe.

The same scene as her first surgery—big red incision, tubes, wires, ventilator, tin foil oxygen tent, beeping machines, and so on—we were prepared for it. We were not prepared, however, for what came along with the extra complications. Every half hour, the nurse pounded on Joelle's little chest with a rubber percussor—a hollow rubber hammer—to loosen the fluids settling into her lungs. A respiratory therapist came every two hours to give her a breathing treatment and to suction out excess lung fluid through her ventilator-tracheal tube.

A few days of maintaining these treatments with no improvement called for additional measures. In addition to the oxygen she received through the ventilator, Joelle was also put on nitric oxide to aid her lung function … another medicine, another machine to be hooked to. Furthermore, she had a chest tube inserted directly through her rib cage, into her right lung for extra drainage of the fluid collecting in it.

One step forward, three steps back.

Jim and I had entered the hospital nervously on surgery day but optimistically, expecting that we'd be home in a week, praying Joelle wouldn't have to go back on supplemental oxygen. There was no way for us to foresee what Joelle's little body would be up against. I was now back in that familiar valley of the shadow of death—literally. I prayed, "God, *please* just let her live. I don't care about oxygen or whatever equipment she might need. I just want to take her home. I just want her on this earth. I just want her to *live. Please.*"

As I sat in the pediatric ICU beside Joelle, I realized it was Halloween. I stared blankly out the window, daydreaming about the adorable lion costume she would have worn that night for trick-or-treating. Poetically, snow actually began to swirl wildly and frantically from the sky at that very moment. Snow in October is unusual (and unwelcomed) for our region of Pennsylvania. It seemed to signify something. Was it representative of the harsh phase my family was currently going through? Or was it a warning that we should prepare for a bitter metaphorical winter that was just beginning?

No matter what season of life we are in, God is God. It is our prerogative to trust Him and execute His call on our lives, no matter what.

In Acts 1:6–8, the disciples were anxious to know what Jesus had in store for them and the kingdom of Israel after His resurrection. They didn't know in just a few minutes that Jesus would be taken up into heaven before their eyes. They had not yet experienced the baptism of the Holy Spirit coming down upon them like fire. They had no idea that they would be the first Christian evangelists who would develop Christianity for the world, be read about two thousand years later, and be models of faith for all humanity. Neither did they know that they would be persecuted, tortured, isolated, and rejected by men, as Jesus was before them. But Jesus knew all of this.

MOLLY HANKEY

He said to them "It is not for you to know times or seasons that the Father has fixed by his own authority. But you will receive power when the Holy Spirit has come upon you, and you will be my witnesses in Jerusalem and in all Judea and Samaria, and to the end of the earth."
(Acts 1:7–8 ESV)

Our seasons and futures are only for the Father to know. He will empower us by His Spirit for every stage of the game. What a promise that is to cling to! Journal your prayer to the Holy Spirit. Ask Him to fill you with His power and whatever else you specifically need in your heart: peace, love, understanding, grace, forgiveness ... The list is unending, as is the power He has for you.

_____

_____

_____

_____

_____

_____

_____

_____

_____

_____

_____

22

Empty No More

One evening after a particularly difficult day for Joelle during the recovery from her second surgery, Jim and I were mindlessly consuming our dinner at the Ronald McDonald House. I was completely exhausted—physically, emotionally, mentally, and spiritually. I was empty, and it must have shown through my whole being. When I thanked a woman from that evening's volunteer group for the meal they provided, she asked if she could pray with me. I welcomed it.

The soft-spoken, silver-haired woman held my hand and gently prayed to our Lord while I unsuccessfully choked back tears. She prayed for a minute or two, then embraced me in a hug in which I could feel the love of Christ overcome me. She gave me hope.

I don't know her name, what group she was with, or where she was from. I do know that God sent her to me at the perfect moment to speak calming peace and hope back into my heart. She prayed strength and spirit back into my mind, body, and soul. God used her as the vessel to fill me up when I was empty.

First Kings 17:7–24 tells the story of a widow and her son who God rescued from starvation and also death from an illness, in His most appropriate timing.

This woman had only enough flour and oil in her jars for one more meager meal. As mothers do, I can imagine she was giving up her own portions of bread in order to sustain her growing son. The woman must have been rationing her baking goods most conservatively over the previous days and weeks so as to prolong her family's survival. She was most likely weak with hunger and emotionally, mentally, and spiritually exhausted as the prophet Elijah found her outside her home, gathering sticks to make a fire for baking what she thought would be her last meal before certain death from starvation. She needed a miracle.

God sent Elijah to her in His perfect timing and miraculously kept her jars, her body, and her soul from becoming empty.

God sends us what we need, exactly when we really need it, according to His purpose. He will never fail us.

Are you empty—or nearly there? Recall a previous time in your life when God came through with sustenance when you most needed it. Do you believe that He will not fail you now?

_____

_____

_____

_____

_____

_____

_____

_____

_____

MOLLY HANKEY

23

Divine Detour

Rounding out week two postsurgery, Joelle's recovery was progressing, but she was still far from being herself. Her shining personality was buried deep inside; she was continuously miserable and difficult to satisfy.

Among other tubes and wires, Joelle had a nasogastric feeding tube in her nose and a central intravenous line stitched into her neck. The doctors were not ready for her to eat or drink at this point, as they wanted to control her liquid intake because of the fluid still in her lungs. The central line in her neck was for the still numerous round-the-clock medications she was receiving.

As "chance" would have it, the pediatric ICU had intercepted some new patients with contagious illnesses. Thankfully now, the new PICU at that hospital has individual rooms. At the time of Joelle's surgeries, the beds were all lined up in the same room, about eight feet apart. This was dangerous for Joelle in her state of recovery, so they decided to move her to another unit where she would have a private, isolated room.

Enter God's divine detour.

Somehow during the move, Joelle's central IV line in her neck came loose. This was a scary disaster; frantic nurses dove over each other to plug the wound and yelled for interns to bring whatever they could find to help stop the bleeding. Eventually the situation came under control, but they couldn't reinsert the IV into her neck; they'd have to insert a line in her arm. This was bad news according to the medical team, but God knew differently.

After the initial screaming torture of stitching up her neck and inserting a new IV into Joelle's arm, she immediately started becoming her happy self again and took a huge step in recovery. Her demeanor improved along with the numbers on all of her monitors. Her blood-oxygen level started climbing right along with her spirits.

The next day, she was moved to an intermediate step-down unit, as her care no longer required the intensive monitoring. On the way to the second new unit in two days, Joelle decided she didn't like the feeding tube in her nose and yanked it right out. "Not cool" by the nurse's reaction, but again, God knew differently.

With Joelle now energetic enough to be squirmy, the tube would be a challenge to reinsert. Consequently, her team decided it was time for some real food and drink. When the clear liquid diet arrived on the meal tray, I didn't think much of it. Unpredictably, I had never seen beef broth make a child so happy! Food was the kick she needed to round third base and head home on her path to discharge.

So often, we think we know what is best and right. We know how to get from point A to B. We've got paths and protocols, for very good and proven reasons. But only God knows what is truly best for us and can see beyond our limited scope. Sometimes He takes us on surprise detours that seem counterproductive and oppositional.

Paul's 275 shipmates in Acts 27–28 experienced a surprise detour when they aimed to sail a short and direct forty miles from Fair Havens to Phoenix but ended up in a wild, windy nightmare and eventually shipwrecked on the island of Malta. These disastrous three and a half months spent with Paul on the stormy sea and shipwrecked on an island, witnessing the miraculous saving grace of God, was a divinely directed detour that I'm sure instilled an eternal faith in Jesus in many of those men. An oppositional wind was what saved their souls in eternity.

Our Father divinely intervenes when we don't even know something needs fixed. Sometimes it's scary walking through it—when the seas are high and the boat is sinking, or nurses are frenzied and your baby is screaming—but He's always working behind the scenes. He divinely detours our humanly planned routes and goals to bring our souls closer to Him.

Perhaps what you are going through right now is a detour that God engineered. Maybe your originally planned course was fine enough, but maybe God has an extraordinary purpose in the recourse you're in. Alternate routes are usually more difficult, slower, and definitely not as convenient, but there is often great value in the journey. Sometimes we can't see that until we have made it to the destination; sometimes we are granted wisdom to appreciate the significance while we are still on the voyage. Can you see the Lord's hand in the course you are on? Is it a course that you designed or one that has been divinely detoured?

_____

_____

_____

_____

_____

_____

_____

_____

_____

_____

_____

_____

24

COMPARISON-ITIS

Discharge day! Day twenty-one—finally time to go home. Wires unhooked, tubes out, no supplemental oxygen needed (thank You, Lord!). Solid food eaten, street clothes on, feet on the floor ... knees buckling, body on the floor, can't stand up. *Now what is wrong with my kid?*

Thrilled with the outcome of the surgery from a cardiology standpoint, ecstatic to see Joelle's blood-oxygen level up again, and beyond thankful that she didn't need to go home with any attachments, we were on cloud nine. Then this unexpected impediment slapped us in the face.

Bedridden for twenty-one days and weak from the trauma of open-heart surgery, Joelle lost all muscle tone in her legs and core. She would require extensive physical and occupational therapy to regain it. *We didn't see that coming.*

Three steps forward and one big step back. With the low muscle tone she had exhibited even before her surgery, this new loss of muscle was exaggerated.

For the next ten months, Joelle had twice-a-week therapy sessions. She learned to stand, crawl, and walk all over again. She got custom orthotic braces for her feet to align her gait and build her leg muscles. We turned every mundane activity into a gross motor exercise.

While her similar-aged friends and cousins were climbing, jumping, riding tricycles, and zipping along, Joelle was unstable standing and walking and lacked any amount of endurance. My mind started down a dark and dangerous path of unfairly comparing her abilities with other children, and into my heart crept a woeful jealousy. I so badly wanted for her a normal childhood and for her to be able to explore the world without falling down a hundred times a day. I knew it was wrong and completely ungrateful after all she had been through, but the roots had grown deep and gripped my heart. I had a *bad* case of comparison-itis, and I wrestled with being grateful and being covetous and even resentful for a very long time. I kept my heart as hidden as I could, from everyone, because I knew I was wrong.

Funny thing was Joelle had no idea that she couldn't do what other kids could. She had no idea that she was physically delayed. It didn't bother her one bit to see others running and romping while she lagged behind them and stumbled and fumbled.

Slowly, and only by God's grace, I realized how Joelle was differently-abled. I realized how He had gifted her with special abilities and interests that were just hers. I was so concerned with her meeting milestones and catching up that I failed to focus on the amazing gifts that God had given solely to her.

How could I have been so ungrateful and so blind?

I knew my heart harbored sinful sentiments. I tried to rid of them myself, but I couldn't do it myself. I didn't want anyone, not even my husband, to see the ugly I was hiding deep inside. That was a mistake. While I was masking my heart and my hurt, the sinful feelings were growing and pushing me downward. I needed someone to help me back up. Thankfully, the Lord showed me I needed to open up, and my family helped me to open my eyes and right my heart.

> If one falls down, his friend can help him up. But pity the
> man who falls and has no one to help him up! Though
> one may be overpowered, two can defend themselves. A
> cord of three strands is not quickly broken.
> (Ecclesiastes 4:10, 12 NIV)

Three strands—the third being God. Two believers wrapping themselves around God in prayer. That's some powerful rope right there.

Are you wrestling with bitter emotions, knowing they are wrong? Don't harbor them. Masking doesn't help. Hiding doesn't help. Muscling through on your own doesn't help! I've been there. I've done all of it! God gave us community and relationships to help us overcome sin and despair. Choose a wise, trustworthy person to share your feelings with, asking them to help you prayerfully right those wrongs in your heart.

_____

_____

_____

_____

_____

_____

_____

_____

_____

_____

_____

_____

_____

25

AT HIS FEET AGAIN

Flash forward. At three and a half years old, Joelle became a big sister to our second daughter, Chaya. Joelle's physicality was in good shape. She was smart as a whip and happy as a lark. I had no anxiety associated with this second pregnancy. By now, I had motherhood experience under my belt, was more relaxed, and was totally ready to handle life with another baby. Chaya came into this world one month early but quickly and easily, and we were all peaceful, content, and blissful … for two weeks.

Around 9:00 p.m. on the day she was two weeks old, Chaya became pale and stopped breathing. As Jim raced us to the local hospital's emergency room, I sat in the back seat of the car with Chaya, flicking her feet and her ribs with my fingers, instigating her to take breaths. In the ER, her respiratory rate was normalized with supplemental oxygen and some medications that have escaped my memory. With no pediatric ICU there, she was airlifted to the children's hospital where she was born, where we had spent so much time with Joelle. Diagnosed with pneumonia, Chaya was treated, and we came home in three days, on the mend.

Not a full two weeks later, she had a repeat episode, but the pneumonia came back with a vengeance. My grandmother was spending the day with me, and as she raced us to the local ER, I breathed breath into Chaya's nose and mouth. In the ER, supplemental oxygen didn't do the trick in reviving her breathing, and her blood-oxygen saturation plummeted to 40 percent. She turned blue, her heartbeat became weak, and her body went totally limp. Frantic doctors and nurses bustled around the room, trying unsuccessfully to medicate and intubate my newborn daughter, to put her on a ventilator.

She was quickly dying.

My only thought as I stared with bleary eyes and shaking hands was *I am going to lose my child … I am going to be a mother who lives this life with only the memory of this baby.*

Thankfully, our pediatrician arrived at the hospital. He sprinted down the hallway to Chaya's room and took charge of the pandemonium. With his God-given talent and skill, he brought my daughter's body back to life.

Again she was airlifted to the children's hospital with the PICU, but this time was not a three-day stay. Her condition was much worse than the first time, and she had experienced trauma in the ER with the unsuccessful first attempts at intubating.

Day after day on a ventilator, receiving umpteen medications and treatments but with no improvement to her condition, I prayed over her and pleaded with Jesus at His feet to heal my dying daughter.

I couldn't believe this was happening to us again; I couldn't believe we were going through another literal valley of the shadow of death with another child. *Why? What is the purpose this time? Have we not suffered enough? What now? God brought us through all the turmoil with Joelle's health just to have us come back to the same fight with Chaya?*

Jarius, falling at Jesus's feet, pleaded earnestly with Him, "My little daughter is dying. Please come and put your hands on her so that she will be healed and live" (Mark 5:22–23 NIV) (paraphrase mine).

I didn't even have to memorize that verse. It was my own prayer, the same prayer of Jarius, the same prayer I prayed for Joelle eighteen months prior, the same prayer of every parent who lacks control over the deteriorating health of their child.

No situation is new for God or out of His realm of care. As isolated as you may feel, you are not alone in it. Whatever your trial is, someone has walked through it before, and God has handled it before. This world is a broken place, but God uses the brokenness for our benefit, in bringing us to His feet. Painful, yes, but purposeful.

Through Him we have also obtained access by faith into this grace in which we stand, and we rejoice in hope of the glory of God. Not only that, but we rejoice in our sufferings, knowing that suffering produces endurance, and endurance produces character, and character produces hope. (Romans 5:2–4 ESV)

You may have little strength left; use whatever you have of it to grasp tightly to your faith. Cling to God's promise to *you*. His glory will prevail, and through your suffering, you will eventually again find hope.

As you meditate on Romans 5:2–4, ask the Holy Spirit to minister to your soul. What is He saying to you? What promises of God's will you anchor yourself to?

_____

_____

_____

_____

_____

_____

_____

_____

_____

_____

26

FULL CIRCLE

Around day ten of Chaya's three-week stay in the PICU, I noticed a first-time mom roaming the halls. She had newborn twins; one of them was born with a congenital heart defect and was being cared for in the PICU-cardio unit. My heart ached for her, as she was experiencing the same exact story I had just a few short years before with Joelle, and she was exhibiting the same exact somber and distraught emotions over her fragile child.

Too familiar. I didn't want the flood of that pain to surface again, as I had successfully put it away and was now dealing with a new round of heartache with Chaya. *It's too much reach out to this woman. I need to distance myself from that. I can't handle it now. I'm not ready to open up about that yet. It's too soon.* Of course, God had a different idea.

Joelle, my mother, and I were having lunch in the family lounge where, by chance, this woman was visiting with her mother simultaneously.

"Talk to her," my mom urged in a whisper.

"No. I'm not ready," I said as my heart pounded and my voice wavered at the thought of what that emotional conversation would consist of. I continued helping Joelle with a puzzle she was putting together. As anxious thoughts raced through my head about Joelle's history, Chaya's current condition, my own unstable emotions, and this distressed new mom sitting a few feet away, something incredible happened. Totally unplanned by me, words came forth unexpectedly from my mouth as I turned toward this lady, as if someone else was in control of my body. "Hi there. I've seen you around, and I think you're the one with the heart baby?" *What is happening? What am I doing?*

She nodded, doing her best to put on a polite little smile through her distress. "I've got a newborn down the hall from you in the PICU, but I wanted to tell you that this"—I put my arm around Joelle—"is *my* heart baby." The woman's and her mother's faces both exhibited shock, joy, confusion, and gratification all at the same time.

Well, I guess I'm doing this! I had Joelle show them her sternal scar, and the tears started rolling down the new mom's face as she looked at Joelle in amazement. "I'm sorry. I didn't mean to upset you," I said. "I just wanted to give you hope that things will get better."

She shook her head in several different directions, trying to communicate with nods as she was totally choked up. Her mother spoke for her with a sweet voice of gratitude and amazement and tears in her eyes. "Thank you *so much* for sharing that with us. We have been praying for some hope and comfort, and you don't know how much this means to us."

There was much more conversation, a fast forever friendship forged, and peaceful hearts in healing that afternoon. God brought Crystal and me together, as much as I resisted opening up my heart initially. Talking to her about experiences with Joelle, answering her questions, and helping her through the same familiar phase brought peace and healing to my heart I didn't even know I needed—peace and healing I didn't even know existed. On the flip side, it was the hope for her healing heart that she had been praying for.

Obviously, I didn't have that conversation on my own. I wish I could say I had the courage to put my heart out there and step up in someone's time of need, but the Holy Spirit handled that one, as God held my heart and melded pieces of it back together. I am incredibly grateful for that.

In that moment, God brought me around full circle from where I started with Joelle's diagnosis: from feeling alone and hopeless when Jim and I wrote that first prayer request email, through leaning on Amy who had gone through it with her child, to now being the one to offer hope and comfort to Crystal. His works are so complete!

When God presents you with the chance, be courageous and offer hope to someone else in need. *Both of you* may need it more than you realize.

> Have I not commanded you? Be strong and courageous. Do not be afraid; do not be discouraged, for the Lord your God will be with you wherever you go. (Joshua 1:9 NIV)

27

LETTING GO

Somewhere along the way, I learned that I had to let go of my dearest possession. Joelle was that. Don't misunderstand; my children are a part of me and will always be. But at one point, I clung to my baby more tightly than I was clinging to my Lord. It's a devious sin, and in the world's secular culture, it's justifiable. By God's commands, it's not.

There are countless biblical anecdotes warning us against treasuring anything else more than God. God blesses and entrusts us as parents with the lives of our children, but they are in fact His to give us and His to take away. They are not our possessions to cling to.

I had to learn to give Joelle to God *completely*, even if it meant her life. I had to learn that I will cherish every day He gives me with her, and if He takes her home before He takes me, I will not question His plan or purpose. *Of course* my heart would be shattered, but it will never be irreparable, because I will forever be honoring Jesus, the ultimate healer.

In Genesis 22, Abraham experienced a much greater, unfathomable parallel. God tested Abraham by commanding him to sacrifice his long-awaited, inconceivably treasured son, Isaac, whom Abraham was grooming to carry on his namesake and inherit his domain. Put yourself in Abraham's shoes. Imagine the pure agony of leading your beloved child on a journey, walking with him, all the while thinking that you would have to painfully kill him, yourself, in order to obey the Living God. Unconscionable!

Thank the good Lord He doesn't test us like that now. But be very honest with yourself. Are you gripping onto something or someone, more tightly than you are gripping onto God? Are you clinging to a relationship, a lifestyle, or even a well-intended desire more closely than you are clinging to Jesus?

God of course spared Isaac's life and honored Abraham for His faithfulness and obedience. He will honor you, too, when you give *everything* to Him.

28

THE UNTHINKABLE

I know that not all stories end up with a living child or loved one. Yours might not …

I am so deeply sorry if that happens or has happened to you. There are no words to express my most sincere sympathy and sorrow. As I have come close to feeling the pain of losing a child, and I've been close to others who have walked through it, I have never experienced that deeply immense, indescribable anguish. There are no words *I* would attempt to offer you that could lessen your heartbreak.

We will never know why God calls children and babies home to Him without letting them live a full, joyful life here on earth. Only He has that answer.

The encouragement I *can* give and I *know* is right is that God *is* good, and God *is* loving—even if He has called your child home. Don't let go of God. Cling to Him, follow Him, and trust Him to heal your heart.

Your loved one is living with Jesus in heaven. You will see your precious one again someday, if you embrace Jesus's gift of salvation and follow Him. Let your incredible, immeasurable loss bring you closer to Jesus.

I've adopted Psalm 143 as my prayer in the midst of deep depression, anxiety, and all loss of hope and joy. Let David's words be planted in your heart as your prayer to the Lord:

Psalm 143 (NIV)—A psalm of David
Lord, hear my prayer,
listen to my cry for mercy;
in your faithfulness and righteousness
come to my relief.
Do not bring your servant into judgment,
for no one living is righteous before you.
The enemy pursues me,
he crushes me to the ground;
he makes me dwell in the darkness
like those long dead.
So my spirit grows faint within me;
my heart within me is dismayed.
I remember the days of long ago;
I meditate on all your works
and consider what your hands have done.
I spread out my hands to you;
I thirst for you like a parched land.
Answer me quickly, O Lord;
my spirit fails.
Do not hide your face from me
or I will be like those who go down to the pit.
Let the morning bring me word of your unfailing love,
for I have put my trust in you.
Show me the way I should go,
for to you I entrust my life.
Rescue me from my enemies, Lord,
for I hide myself in you.
Teach me to do your will,
for you are my God;
may your good Spirit
lead me on level ground.
For your name's sake, Lord, preserve my life;
in your righteousness, bring me out of trouble.
In your unfailing love, silence my enemies;
destroy all my foes,
for I am your servant.

MOLLY HANKEY

29

OUR STORY IS HIS GLORY

God has used our family's narrative to show His divine glory. Through Joelle's heart, He has reached others well beyond our family with His encouragement, consolation, and inspiration.

Our now retired pastor used Joelle's miraculous life as illustrations in his sermons. We have been able to share with our church congregation, in our workplaces, and multiple other avenues the powerful blessings of God and the result of powerful prayers.

Joelle is now eleven years old and in sixth grade. As she became old enough to understand, we taught her to celebrate her special heart, knowing that God made her perfectly the way He wanted her. We are teaching her to embrace her story and use it as a tool in telling others of God's amazing power and grace. The good Lord not only gave her a "special heart," but paired with it a heart for evangelism, as well as a love of speaking and a natural affinity for the spotlight!

Joelle is different, and she knows it. And best of all, she's happy about it. Over the past several years, she has participated with the Kids Heart Challenge Campaign through her public school and the American Heart Association. Because of our incredibly gracious family's and friends' awareness of her ongoing medical battle, as well as her convincingly charming pitch for donations, Joelle has been the top fundraiser in the region several times over and has been recognized in a school-wide assembly, among other things. She has been able to speak to her school about God, how He has given her a special heart and how she is being cared for.

Joelle was recently selected by the American Heart Association to be our state ambassador for the Kids with Heart program, which engages young heart disease patients and survivors in the mission of inspiring others to live healthier lives by sharing their personal stories. As such, she will have opportunities to speak at schools, events and through media, sharing her journey and testimony. We cannot wait to see what God has in store for this role, and trust He has soil prepared for the seeds she will plant.

Twelve years ago, I prayed for God to heal my daughter's heart. Instead, He has healed mine. He created her for a greater purpose that I could not see. He created our story for His glory.

God created a special plan and purpose for *your* adversities: to further His kingdom, to glorify His name, and to bring *you* closer to Him in the process. What a wild and rough ride it may be, but take heart! *You are not alone.* He will hold your hand the whole way if you ask Him to and seek His face.

> "For I know the plans I have for you," declares the Lord, "plans to prosper you and not to harm you, plans to give you hope and a future. Then you will call upon me and come and pray to me, and I will listen to you. You will seek me and find me when you seek me with all your heart."
> (Jeremiah 29: 11–13 NIV)

Over the years, I have come back again and again to the story of Jesus healing a blind man. The disciples wondered why the man was born this way. Was it a result of sin? No. Jesus's words: "This happened so that the works of God might be displayed in him. As long as it is day, we must do the works of Him who sent me" (John 9:1–4a NIV) (paraphrase mine.) The words here of Jesus Christ Himself give me absolute confirmation that my daughter was born like this for His purpose. And I was chosen to help carry that purpose out.

If your vision is dimmed by overcoming shadows, cling to the fact that God doesn't want you to stay there. He wants you to walk in His light, and He will bring you into it; keep your eyes on Him. He has a bigger and better purpose for you than walking in shadows.

Your story is His glory.

> Whatever you do, do it with all your heart.
> (Colossians 3:23 NLV)

About the Author

Molly Hankey is a life-long Christ follower who seeks to help fellow believers strengthen their faith in God and deepen their relationship with Jesus. She wrote Hearts in Healing in obedience to the Holy Spirit's calling and honors Him with all acknowledgement for the content of the book. Molly lives in Pennsylvania with her husband and their two daughters. The family enjoys serving together in their church and being outdoors enjoying God's creation.

Connect with the author:
Facebook @heartsinhealingdevo
or
heartsinhealingdevo@gmail.com

Printed in the United States
by Baker & Taylor Publisher Services